THE ALGORITHM'S MUSE

How TikTok's BookTok Community Redefined Literary Success and Made Romantasy Rule

Azirion Jase

Independently published

ASIN: B0F7XZQHMQ

ISBN: 9798282906813

Imprint: Independently published.

CONTENTS

INTRODUCTION

The Algorithm's Muse

It starts, as it so often does, with a phone screen. A 15-second video: a reader, eyes wide, clutching a book to their chest, tears welling. Overlaid text screams, "YOU NEED TO READ THIS NOW." A trending sound, melancholic yet hopeful, plays in the background. Within hours, this snippet, a raw, emotional reaction to a fantasy novel brimming with dragons, forbidden magic, and a slow-burn romance, is liked thousands of times. Within days, it's millions. The book, perhaps a debut from an unknown author or a forgotten gem from a publisher's backlist, rockets onto bestseller charts. Bookstores scramble to order copies; rights sell in multiple countries. This isn't a carefully orchestrated marketing campaign from a major publishing house. This is BookTok. This is the algorithm's muse in action, a digital whisper network turned global kingmaker, and its current obsession is "Romantasy."

This book, *The Algorithm's Muse: How TikTok's BookTok Community Redefined Literary Success and Made Romantasy Rule*, delves into this extraordinary cultural and commercial phenomenon. We stand at the confluence of rapidly evolving social media landscapes, shifting reader preferences, and a publishing industry in constant flux. The rise of "Romantasy"— a captivating blend of romance and fantasy—along with a broader surge in related Speculative Fiction genres like Dystopian Romance, Mythological Retellings, and Dark Academia, isn't merely a passing trend; it signifies a seismic shift in how books are discovered, consumed, and culturally valued. At the heart of this transformation is BookTok, a vibrant subcommunity on the social media platform TikTok. This global, user-driven collective has become an undeniable powerhouse, its influence rewriting the rules of literary success and challenging long-held notions of what constitutes "literary value." While the digital landscape of BookTok is ever-evolving, this analysis focuses on a particularly formative and explosive period: roughly from early 2022 to early 2025, a time when the platform's impact on the literary world became undeniable and its patterns of influence solidified.

To understand the meteoric ascent of BookTok-driven genres, we must consider the fertile ground from which they sprang. Socially, the early 2020s, marked by global uncertainties and a deep-seated yearning for connection and escapism, created a hunger for immersive narratives that offer both grand adventures and profound emotional resonance. Technologically, TikTok's unique algorithmic architecture, with its unparalleled ability to personalize content and propel niche interests into mainstream awareness, provided the perfect vehicle for these stories to find their audience. Simultaneously, the publishing industry, already navigating the rise of independent authorship and the changing dynamics of book marketing, found itself presented with both an unprecedented opportunity and a formidable challenge: to adapt to a world where a 60-second video could dictate tomorrow's bestsellers.

Therefore, this book argues that TikTok's BookTok community has fundamentally reshaped the contemporary fiction landscape, acting as a powerful and unprecedented catalyst for the "Romantasy" and broader Speculative Fiction surge. It has achieved this by leveraging emotionally resonant, visually driven user-generated content and algorithmic amplification to create viral bestsellers, cultivate dedicated global fan communities, and elevate new and diverse authorial voices. More than just a marketing tool, BookTok's success reflects and responds to a collective cultural yearning for immersive escapism intertwined with intense emotional narratives and a sense of shared experience. In doing so, it is not only changing what we read but is also prompting a critical re-evaluation of traditional notions of literary value and success, forcing us to ask new questions about who gets to decide what makes a book important.

Our journey through this fascinating landscape will unfold across several key explorations. We will begin by dissecting The Rise of the Algorithm's Muse: Understanding BookTok's Ecosystem (Chapter 1), examining the platform mechanics and content conventions that make BookTok such a potent force for literary discovery. Next, in Dragons, Desire, and Dark Academia: Deconstructing the Appeal of Viral Genres (Chapter 2), we will delve into the specific literary elements, tropes, and themes within Romantasy and its related speculative fiction cousins that captivate millions, critically assessing their appeal and narrative power. Chapter 3, From Viral Videos to Bestseller Lists: BookTok's Remaking of Authorship and Publishing, will investigate the profound impact on authors and the publishing industry, from the rise of indie sensations to the adaptation of traditional marketing strategies. We will then explore the vibrant communities that fuel these trends in #BookTokMadeMeReadIt: Community, Fandom, and Participatory Culture (Chapter 4), analyzing how shared passion translates into collective action and cultural identity. Finally, Chapter 5, Beyond the Hype: What the Romantasy Craze Tells Us About Modern Readership and Culture, will interpret this phenomenon as a mirror reflecting contemporary anxieties, desires, and the evolving definition of literary engagement in an algorithmically mediated world, paying particular attention to whether BookTok primarily reflects pre-existing desires or actively shapes new ones.

In approaching this subject, my perspective is one of critical appreciation. As a keen observer of cultural trends and the ever-evolving relationship between media, technology, and storytelling, I aim to provide an analysis that is both rigorous and accessible. This book seeks to understand the BookTok phenomenon in its full complexity—celebrating its democratizing potential and the joy it brings to readers, while also critically examining its commercial dimensions, its impact on literary production, and the broader questions it raises about cultural value in the digital age. The goal is not to definitively praise or condemn, but to illuminate the intricate workings and far-reaching implications of the algorithm's muse and the new literary world it is helping to sculpt.

CHAPTER 1: THE RISE OF THE ALGORITHM'S MUSE

Understanding BookTok's Ecosystem

The literary world has always had its tastemakers: esteemed critics, influential review publications, prestigious awards committees, and the carefully curated shelves of independent bookstores. For decades, these gatekeepers largely shaped which books found their way into the hands of readers and which authors rose to prominence. Then came TikTok, a platform initially synonymous with dance challenges and lip-syncing teenagers. Few would have predicted that this vibrant, fast-paced social media app would birth BookTok, a subcommunity so potent it could catapult obscure novels to international bestseller status overnight, resurrect authors' backlist titles, and fundamentally alter the strategies of global publishing houses. This chapter delves into the intricate ecosystem of BookTok, examining how TikTok's unique platform mechanics and the specific content conventions cultivated by its users have combined to create an unprecedented engine for literary discovery and trendsetting. BookTok's influence is not a mere fluke; it is the product of a sophisticated interplay between algorithmic amplification, raw emotional expression, and community-driven curation that bypasses traditional barriers, forging direct, visceral connections between stories and a vast, engaged audience.

The "Accidental" Kingmaker – How Booktok Emerged

BookTok wasn't a planned feature or a corporate initiative. Like many organic online communities, it blossomed from the grassroots, fueled by the passion of individual users. Its origins can be traced back to the early days of the COVID-19 pandemic, around 2020. As lockdowns swept across the globe, people found themselves with more time for reading and a greater need for connection. TikTok, already a rapidly growing platform, became a space where users could share their experiences and find community. Early book-related content often involved simple recommendations, bookshelf tours, or participation in reading challenges. However, it quickly evolved. Users began to experiment with TikTok's unique features – short-form video, trending sounds, and creative editing tools – to express their love for books in new and compelling ways. Creators like @aymansbooks and @caitsbooks are often cited among the pioneers who helped popularize the #BookTok hashtag, showcasing a more emotionally driven and aesthetically focused approach to book content. What started as a niche interest gradually coalesced into a recognizable subcommunity, its growth accelerated by TikTok's powerful recommendation algorithm, which began to identify and promote this burgeoning content category to an ever-widening audience of book lovers. The term "accidental kingmaker" is apt because neither TikTok nor the publishing industry initially foresaw the sheer scale of influence this user-led movement would come to wield.

The Anatomy Of A Booktok Video: Visuals, Sound,

Emotion, Brevity

A key to understanding BookTok's power lies in the distinct anatomy of its content. Unlike traditional book reviews, which often rely on lengthy prose and critical analysis, BookTok videos are typically short, visceral, and highly visual. Brevity is paramount; most videos range from 15 to 60 seconds, demanding immediate engagement. Visuals are central: a close-up of a stunning cover, an aesthetically pleasing bookshelf ("shelfie"), a time-lapse of someone reading, or, most famously, the creator's own face reacting to a particularly impactful scene. These visuals are often paired with trending sounds or popular music clips that evoke a specific mood – a melancholic piano piece for a tearjerker, an epic orchestral score for a fantasy adventure, or a playful pop song for a lighthearted romance.

However, the true secret ingredient is emotion. BookTok thrives on authentic, often unfiltered, emotional responses. Creators don't just tell you a book is good; they *show* you. They film themselves crying over a tragic ending ("this book shattered me"), laughing at a witty character, gasping at a plot twist, or fanning themselves over a steamy scene. This raw display of feeling creates an immediate, empathetic connection with viewers. It's the digital equivalent of a passionate friend grabbing your arm and insisting, "You *have* to read this." This emotional authenticity, coupled with creative editing – quick cuts, text overlays highlighting key quotes or tropes, and the use of filters – makes for highly shareable and persuasive content. For instance, a video showcasing the "enemies-to-lovers" trope might feature quick snippets of dialogue or scenes from a book, set to a dramatic soundtrack, culminating in the creator's ecstatic reaction, all within 30 seconds. This potent combination of visual appeal, auditory cues, emotional resonance, and conciseness makes BookTok videos incredibly effective at capturing attention and sparking curiosity.

Algorithmic Curation And The "For You Page": How Trends Spread

TikTok's algorithm, particularly its "For You Page" (FYP), is the engine that drives BookTok's extraordinary reach. The FYP is a personalized, endlessly scrolling feed of videos curated for each user based on their interactions – videos liked, shared, commented on, accounts followed, and even the duration of time spent watching specific types of content. Unlike other social media platforms that heavily prioritize content from accounts a user already follows, TikTok's FYP is exceptionally adept at surfacing content from entirely new creators. This is crucial for BookTok's function as a discovery engine.

When a BookTok video starts to gain traction – accumulating likes, comments, shares, and completions (viewers watching the entire video) – the algorithm recognizes this engagement as a signal of quality or interest. It then pushes the video to a wider audience with similar interaction patterns. If these users also engage positively, the video's reach expands exponentially, potentially going viral and appearing on millions of FYPs globally. This algorithmic amplification means that a single heartfelt video from an unknown creator about a niche book can, in theory, achieve massive visibility almost overnight. It's a system that rewards engaging content, regardless of the creator's existing follower count, creating a more democratized pathway to influence compared to traditional media. The algorithm also learns to identify users interested in specific genres or tropes, further refining its recommendations. If you watch several videos about "morally grey anti-heroes" in fantasy novels, expect your FYP to soon be populated with more of the same, creating a powerful feedback loop that can rapidly consolidate interest around particular books or themes, thus birthing a trend. While the precise workings of the algorithm remain a closely guarded secret, its impact is undeniable: it is the invisible hand guiding users to their next favorite read, often with startling accuracy.

Hashtags, Challenges, And Community: Building A Niche At Scale

While the algorithm plays a significant role, BookTok is also actively shaped by its community through the strategic use of hashtags, participation in challenges, and ongoing conversations. Hashtags are the organizational backbone of BookTok. Beyond the primary #BookTok tag (which, as of early 2025, boasts billions upon billions of views), a constellation of more specific tags helps users find and categorize content. These include genre tags (#Romantasy, #DarkAcademia, #SciFiBooks), trope tags (#EnemiesToLovers, #FoundFamily, #OneBedTrope), author tags (#SarahJMaas, #RebeccaYarros), and challenge tags (#ReadingChallenge, #BookTokMadeMeBuyIt). These hashtags not only improve discoverability but also foster a sense of shared identity and interest among users. Searching for #FourthWing, for example, instantly connects a user to a vast library of reviews, fan theories, aesthetic edits, and discussions specifically about that book.

Reading challenges and trends further galvanize the community. These might involve reading a certain number of books in a month, exploring books by diverse authors, or participating in "readalongs" of specific titles. These shared activities create a sense of collective experience and friendly competition, encouraging users to engage more deeply with books and with each other. Furthermore, TikTok's features like "duet" and "stitch" allow users to directly respond to or build upon each other's content, fostering dynamic conversations and collaborative storytelling around books. A creator might post a video asking for recommendations for books with a specific theme, and dozens of others might stitch their own video replies, creating a rich, crowdsourced reading list. This interconnectedness transforms BookTok from a simple collection of individual reviews into a vibrant, interactive cultural space where trends are not just passively consumed but actively co-created and amplified by the community itself, allowing a niche interest to achieve remarkable scale.

The "Authenticity" Factor: Why Booktok Recommendations Resonate

Perhaps the most crucial element underpinning BookTok's influence is the perceived authenticity of its recommendations. In an age of sponsored content and polished marketing campaigns, BookTok recommendations often feel like genuine endorsements from trusted peers. Creators are typically everyday readers sharing their honest, unvarnished opinions and emotional reactions. This peer-to-peer dynamic fosters a level of trust that can be more persuasive than traditional advertising. When a BookToker films themselves genuinely sobbing over a book's ending or excitedly recounting its plot twists, viewers often feel a stronger, more personal connection to the recommendation than they might from a formal review in a literary journal or a publisher's blurb.

This sense of authenticity is further enhanced by the visual intimacy of the platform. Seeing someone's face, their expressions, and their personal environment (often their own bedroom or living room, surrounded by their books) creates a para-social relationship that feels more personal and relatable. While the line between authentic enthusiasm and performance can sometimes blur, especially as creators gain larger followings and potential brand deals, the foundational appeal of BookTok lies in this feeling of shared passion among equals. It's this potent combination of algorithmic reach and the persuasive power of authentic, emotional, peer-driven endorsements that allows BookTok to bypass traditional gatekeepers. It doesn't need the approval of established critics for a book to take off; it needs the impassioned advocacy of its user base, amplified by the platform's powerful recommendation engine.

The ecosystem of BookTok, therefore, is a complex, dynamic interplay of technological affordances and human creativity. TikTok provides the stage, the tools, and the algorithmic spotlight, but it is the users—the readers, the creators, the fans—who write the script, perform the scenes, and ultimately decide which stories deserve a standing ovation. Having established *how* this digital kingmaker operates, identifying the mechanics of its influence from viral video structures to algorithmic curation and the power of authentic community engagement, the stage is now set to explore a crucial question: *what* kinds of books, what specific narratives and tropes, thrive in this unique environment? The next chapter will delve into the heart of Romantasy and its speculative fiction kin, deconstructing their immense appeal and examining why these particular genres have become the darlings of the algorithm's muse.

CHAPTER 2: DRAGONS, DESIRE, AND DARK ACADEMIA

*Deconstructing the Appeal
of Viral Genres*

The previous chapter illuminated the "how" of BookTok's ascendancy—the algorithmic alchemy and community dynamics that turn videos into viral sensations and books into bestsellers. But the most sophisticated discovery engine is only as powerful as the appeal of what it promotes. This chapter ventures into the heart of the "what": the narratives themselves. What is it about Romantasy, with its soaring dragons, intricate magic systems, and heart-stopping romances, that has so thoroughly captivated the BookTok zeitgeist and, by extension, a massive global readership? Furthermore, how do related speculative fiction subgenres—the stark warnings of Dystopian Romance, the scholarly shadows of Dark Academia often infused with fantastical elements, and the reimagined legends of Mythological Retellings—contribute to this literary moment? This chapter argues that the Romantasy and Speculative Fiction genres popularized by BookTok tap into profound and often overlapping reader desires for immersive escapism, high-stakes emotional narratives, wish-fulfillment, and themes of empowerment. They achieve this resonance through the strategic and often comforting deployment of beloved literary tropes, though this very popularity also invites critical discussion regarding genre saturation, formulaic storytelling, and the evolving definitions of literary merit within these rapidly expanding categories.

Defining Romantasy (And Its Cousins): More Than Just Romance In A Fantastical Setting

At its core, "Romantasy" is a portmanteau that elegantly describes its constituent parts: Romance and Fantasy. However, to define it merely as "romance in a fantastical setting" would be an oversimplification, failing to capture the nuanced interplay between its two halves. In successful Romantasy, the romantic plot and the fantastical plot are deeply intertwined, often inextricable. The external conflicts of the fantasy world—wars, political intrigue, magical quests, prophecies—directly impact the development of the romantic relationship, and vice-versa. The stakes of the romance are frequently elevated to world-altering levels, and the challenges faced by the couple are not just personal but have broader implications for the fictional society they inhabit. For example, in Rebecca Yarros's *Fourth Wing*, Violet Sorrengail's struggle to survive the brutal Navarre war college and bond with her dragon is intrinsically linked to her developing, and initially forbidden, relationship with Xaden Riorson, the son of a rebellion leader. Their personal connection becomes a potential catalyst for political upheaval.

While Romantasy currently reigns as the dominant force on BookTok, its popularity has created a halo effect, drawing attention to and often blending with other speculative fiction subgenres that share similar DNA. Dystopian Romance, a well-established category that saw a resurgence, often features protagonists fighting for love and survival against oppressive regimes in bleak future societies (e.g., Tahereh Mafi's *Shatter Me* series, which enjoyed a significant BookTok revival). The high stakes and themes of rebellion resonate with Romantasy readers. Mythological Retellings, such as Madeline Miller's *Circe* or Jennifer Saint's *Ariadne* (though perhaps appealing to a slightly different segment of BookTok), often incorporate strong romantic elements and powerful female protagonists, breathing new life into ancient tales with a contemporary emotional sensibility. Scarlett St. Clair's *A Touch of Darkness* series, a direct Hades and Persephone retelling, leans heavily into Romantasy tropes. Dark Academia, with its atmospheric settings of old universities, secret societies, and pursuit of forbidden knowledge, increasingly incorporates fantastical or supernatural elements and intense, often morally ambiguous relationships, as seen in Olivie Blake's *The Atlas Six*. Based on current BookTok trends and sales data from the 2022-2025 period, Romantasy clearly plays the primary role, with Dystopian Romance and romantically-inclined Mythological Retellings acting as significant, often overlapping, secondary players. Dark Academia with strong romantic and fantastical threads also carves out a notable niche, frequently sharing readership with Romantasy. The common thread is often a potent mix of world-ending stakes and heart-wrenching emotional journeys, all filtered through a lens that prioritizes character agency and intense interpersonal dynamics.

Trope Culture: The Building Blocks Of Booktok Bestsellers

One of the most striking aspects of BookTok's literary discourse is its unabashed celebration of tropes. Far from being seen as clichés, tropes are embraced as beloved narrative building blocks, shorthand for specific emotional experiences and relationship dynamics that readers actively seek out. BookTok creators often make videos specifically dedicated to dissecting, recommending, or humorously portraying favorite tropes, and these become key search terms for readers.

The "Enemies-to-Lovers" trope is arguably the reigning champion of Romantasy on BookTok. The appeal lies in the delicious tension, witty banter, and the eventual, hard-won intimacy that blossoms against a backdrop of initial animosity. The journey from hatred or deep mistrust to passionate love provides a powerful emotional arc. Books like Sarah J. Maas's *A Court of Thorns and Roses* series (specifically Feyre and Rhysand) or Jennifer L. Armentrout's *From Blood and Ash* series are frequently cited exemplars. Viewers revel in the "he falls first and harder" sub-trope or the "who did this to you?" moment of protective fury from a character who was previously an antagonist.

Another pervasive and beloved trope is "Found Family," where a group of unrelated individuals, often outcasts or survivors, come together to form a deep, loyal, and supportive bond that rivals or surpasses biological kinship. In worlds fraught with danger and political instability, the found family offers a haven of acceptance and unwavering support. This resonates deeply with readers seeking connection and belonging. Leigh Bardugo's *Six of Crows* duology, though pre-dating the peak BookTok era, gained renewed massive popularity on the platform partly due to its masterful execution of this trope.

The "Forced Proximity" or "One Bed Trope" is a classic that reliably generates romantic tension and humorous situations, forcing characters who might otherwise avoid each other into close quarters, leading to vulnerability and the breakdown of emotional barriers. Similarly, "Fake Dating/Fake Marriage" provides a framework for characters to develop genuine feelings under the guise of a fabricated relationship. These tropes, while seemingly simple, are powerful vehicles for character development and romantic progression. The appeal of these tropes lies in their familiarity and the promise of a specific kind of emotional payoff. Readers know what they are getting, and they actively seek the comfort and excitement these narrative patterns provide. However, the sheer prevalence of certain tropes can also lead to discussions about market saturation and a potential for formulaic storytelling if not handled with fresh perspectives or unique execution.

Character Archetypes That Captivate: Strong Protagonists, Complex Love Interests

Beyond plot tropes, specific character archetypes consistently capture the BookTok imagination. There's a strong preference for "strong female protagonists" – women who are not merely passive objects of desire but active agents in their own stories. They might be physically capable warriors, magically gifted individuals, or possess sharp intellect and unwavering resolve. Violet in *Fourth Wing*, learning to navigate a brutal world despite her perceived physical frailty, or Aelin Galathynius from Maas's *Throne of Glass* series, exemplify this. This emphasis on female agency is a significant draw for a predominantly female readership.

Equally compelling are the "morally grey love interests" or anti-heroes. These are often powerful, brooding figures with dark pasts, questionable methods, but ultimately, a fierce loyalty and protective instinct towards the protagonist. Characters like Rhysand (ACOTAR) or Xaden Riorson (*FourthWing*) fit this mold. Their complexity, the hint of danger combined with deep-seated devotion (often expressed through the "touch her and you die" sub-trope), makes them irresistible to many readers. The allure lies in the fantasy of being unconditionally loved and protected by someone who possesses formidable power, and perhaps, in the vicarious thrill of taming or understanding a dangerous entity. The dynamic often explores themes of redemption, acceptance, and the idea that love can flourish even in darkness.

World-Building And Escapism: The Allure Of Other Realities

A fundamental appeal of Romantasy and its speculative cousins is the promise of escapism. Intricate world-building is key to this. Readers crave to be transported to richly imagined realms with unique magic systems, distinct cultures, fascinating creatures (dragons being a perennial favorite), and complex political landscapes. Whether it's the dragon-riding academies of Navarre, the fae courts of Prythian, or the shadowy halls of a magical university, these settings offer a complete departure from the mundane. The more detailed and internally consistent the world, the more immersive the reading experience. BookTok videos often highlight the aesthetic qualities of these worlds, creating "mood boards" or "aesthetic edits" that visually represent the feel of a particular book's setting, further enhancing its escapist appeal. This desire for immersive worlds became particularly acute during and after periods of real-world uncertainty and confinement, offering readers a much-needed refuge.

Emotional Intensity: Why These Stories Evoke Such Strong Reactions

At their heart, the books that go viral on BookTok are those that elicit powerful emotional responses. The narratives are often characterized by high emotional stakes: life-or-death situations, epic betrayals, forbidden love, devastating losses, and triumphant victories. Readers aren't just looking for a passively entertaining story; they want to *feel* deeply. As discussed in Chapter 1, BookTok creators excel at conveying these emotions, sharing their tears, gasps, and swoons. This emotional intensity is a core part of the appeal. The books provide a safe space to experience a wide range of powerful emotions, from heartbreak to elation, often in a condensed and cathartic way. The focus on romantic love, with its inherent vulnerability and passion, is a primary driver of this emotional intensity. The journey of the central couple, fraught with obstacles both internal and external, becomes an emotional rollercoaster that readers eagerly invest in.

Critical Reflections: Addressing Potential Homogenization, Superficiality, Or Quality Concerns

While the enthusiasm for these genres is undeniable, the rapid proliferation of BookTok-driven trends also invites critical reflection. One common concern is the potential for genre homogenization. As certain tropes and character archetypes prove immensely popular, there's a risk that authors and publishers might increasingly gravitate towards these proven formulas, leading to a market flooded with similar-sounding stories. This can result in "trope fatigue" among some readers and make it harder for truly innovative or unconventional narratives to break through.

Questions about superficiality or quality also arise. The emphasis on easily digestible, trope-heavy narratives and rapid-fire emotional payoffs can sometimes overshadow deeper thematic exploration or nuanced character development in some popular titles. The speed of trend cycles and the pressure to publish quickly to capitalize on viral moments might also impact editorial rigor. It's important to acknowledge that "popular" does not always equate to "critically acclaimed" by traditional literary standards, and BookTok itself is not a monolith; within the community, there are ongoing discussions and critiques regarding these very issues. Readers debate the merits of different books, call out overused tropes, and express desires for more diversity and originality. This internal critique is a healthy sign of a maturing literary subculture. The challenge, then, is to balance the undeniable joy and community these books foster with a discerning eye for storytelling craft and originality.

The immense appeal of Romantasy and its related speculative fiction genres on BookTok is a multifaceted phenomenon. It stems from their ability to deliver potent doses of escapism through rich world-building, to satisfy deep-seated desires for intense emotional connection and empowerment through compelling character arcs and high-stakes romance, and to offer the comforting familiarity of beloved narrative tropes. These stories are not just light entertainment; they are fulfilling specific emotional and psychological needs for a vast readership. Having deconstructed the elements that make these books so desirable, the next chapter will explore the profound impact this desirability, amplified by BookTok, has had on authors and the traditional structures of the publishing industry, effectively rewriting the rules of literary success.

CHAPTER 3: FROM VIRAL VIDEOS TO BESTSELLER LISTS

BookTok's Remaking of
Authorship and Publishing

T he journey from a fleeting 15-second video to the coveted top spot on international bestseller lists is a narrative that has become astonishingly common in the BookTok era. Chapters 1 and 2 explored the mechanics of BookTok's influence and the inherent appeal of the genres it champions. Now, we turn our attention to the profound, often disruptive, consequences of this phenomenon for the very structure of the literary world. This chapter investigates how BookTok's unparalleled ability to generate organic, viral enthusiasm for books has fundamentally altered traditional publishing models, created unprecedented pathways to success for authors (particularly independent and debut voices), and compelled a centuries-old industry to rapidly adapt its strategies for acquisition, marketing, and reader engagement. This chapter argues that BookTok has democratized certain aspects of literary success by providing a platform for authors and backlist titles to gain massive visibility, thereby challenging established gatekeeping mechanisms and forcing publishers to become more agile and responsive to digitally-native trends and direct reader feedback. However, this rapid evolution is not without its complexities, presenting new challenges regarding sustainability, authorial pressure, and the very definition of quality in a market increasingly driven by viral velocity.

The New Gatekeepers: How Booktok Influences Acquisitions And Marketing

For decades, the path to publication was largely controlled by a series of established gatekeepers: literary agents meticulously sifting through query letters, acquisition editors at publishing houses making calculated bets on manuscripts, and marketing departments strategizing traditional promotional campaigns. BookTok has not entirely dismantled this structure, but it has undeniably introduced a powerful new variable, and in some cases, a formidable new gatekeeper: the collective voice of its user base. Publishers are no longer solely reliant on internal assessments or traditional review outlets to gauge a book's potential. They are now keenly observing BookTok trends, tracking viral sounds associated with specific books, and monitoring which titles are generating organic buzz.

This has led to a discernible shift in acquisition strategies. Books that explode on BookTok, even those initially self-published or from very small presses, are increasingly being snapped up by major publishing houses for wider distribution, often with significant advances. Lauren Roberts' *Powerless*, initially an indie success story fueled by BookTok, secured a traditional publishing deal with Simon & Schuster, illustrating this trend. Similarly, backlist titles—books published years, sometimes decades, prior—can experience astonishing resurgences. Colleen Hoover's extensive backlist, for example, saw unprecedented sales spikes years after initial publication, largely driven by sustained BookTok enthusiasm. Marketing departments, too, are scrambling to adapt. Traditional advertising, while still present, is often supplemented or even overshadowed by efforts to engage with the BookTok community. This includes sending advance reader copies (ARCs) directly to influential BookTok creators, collaborating on sponsored content (though transparency here is key and sometimes debated), and even encouraging their own authors to build a TikTok presence. The speed is also a factor; publishers are learning they must react quickly to emerging trends, as the BookTok spotlight can shift with dizzying rapidity. This reactive stance, while necessary, can also strain traditional publishing timelines, which are typically much slower.

Indie Author Breakthroughs: Bypassing The Traditional Path

One of the most celebrated impacts of BookTok is its potential to elevate independent authors, allowing them to bypass the traditional gatekeeping process entirely and connect directly with a massive audience. Before BookTok, self-published authors often faced an uphill battle for visibility, relying on platforms like Amazon's Kindle Direct Publishing and meticulous, often costly, self-promotion. While success was possible, achieving breakout bestseller status was rare. BookTok has changed that calculus. Authors who understand the platform's culture and can create engaging content around their books—or whose books organically resonate with BookTok creators—can find themselves with viral hits on their hands.

The story of Olivie Blake's *The Atlas Six* is a prime example. Initially self-published, the dark academia fantasy gained such immense popularity on BookTok that it sparked a fierce bidding war among traditional publishers, eventually being acquired by Tor Books. This demonstrates a significant power shift: instead of authors pitching to publishers, publishers are now, in some instances, chasing authors who have already proven their market viability through BookTok success. This offers immense hope and opportunity for unagented or debut authors who might have been overlooked by the traditional system. It allows for a more direct author-to-reader connection, where the primary intermediaries are the platform's algorithm and the community of fellow readers. However, this path also demands a new set of skills from authors, including content creation, social media engagement, and often, managing the business side of their sudden success.

The Author As Creator: Building A Platform On Tiktok

The rise of BookTok has also redefined, for many, what it means to be an author in the digital age. Increasingly, authors are not just writers but also content creators and community managers. Building a personal platform on TikTok can be a powerful tool for connecting with readers, promoting new releases, and offering a behind-the-scenes glimpse into their writing lives. Authors like Rebecca Yarros (*Fourth Wing*, *Iron Flame*) have cultivated significant TikTok followings, engaging directly with fans, answering questions, and sharing their enthusiasm for their own work and the genres they write in. This direct engagement can foster a loyal readership and create a sense of intimacy between author and fan that was previously much harder to achieve.

However, this expectation—or perceived necessity—for authors to be active and adept on social media also presents challenges. Not all authors are comfortable with or skilled at content creation, and the pressure to maintain an engaging online presence can detract from writing time and add significant emotional labor. There are also concerns that authors might feel compelled to tailor their work to fit prevailing BookTok trends or to project a certain persona to gain visibility. The authenticity that BookTok values can become a performance, and the line between genuine interaction and self-marketing can blur. Furthermore, the direct line of communication, while often positive, can also expose authors to negative feedback, online harassment, or unrealistic fan expectations, adding another layer of pressure to their public-facing role.

Publishers Playing Catch-Up: Strategies, Adaptations, And Challenges

Traditional publishing houses, initially caught somewhat off-guard by the velocity and impact of BookTok, are now actively working to integrate the platform into their operational strategies. This involves more than just marketing. Editorial departments are paying closer attention to the tropes, themes, and pacing that resonate on BookTok when considering acquisitions or providing developmental feedback. Sales teams are using BookTok data to forecast demand and manage print runs, though the unpredictability of viral trends can still lead to stock shortages or, conversely, overprinting if a trend fades quickly.

One notable adaptation is the increased production of special editions and BookTok-focused book boxes. Recognizing the BookTok community's appreciation for aesthetically pleasing physical books, publishers are releasing editions with features like sprayed edges, custom endpapers, foiled covers, and bonus content, often targeted directly at this engaged readership. Subscription boxes curated around BookTok trends or specific popular authors have also flourished. While these initiatives cater effectively to consumer demand and create new revenue streams, they also contribute to a culture of collectability that can sometimes prioritize the physical object over the literary content itself. Publishers also face the challenge of authenticity; attempts to manufacture viral moments or co-opt BookTok trends in a way that feels inauthentic to the community are often met with skepticism or derision. The most successful publisher strategies involve genuine collaboration with BookTok creators and a deep understanding of the platform's organic nature. A significant challenge remains the speed and unpredictability of BookTok; what's viral today might be forgotten tomorrow, making long-term planning difficult for an industry accustomed to more extended production cycles.

The Economics Of Booktok: Sales, Special Editions, And New Revenue Streams

The economic impact of BookTok is undeniable. Books featured prominently on the platform regularly dominate bestseller lists, including the *New York Times* and *USA Today*. Authors like Sarah J. Maas and Rebecca Yarros have seen their sales figures reach astronomical heights, driven in large part by BookTok's sustained enthusiasm. This translates not only into significant revenue for authors and publishers but also has a ripple effect on bookstores, both independent and chain, which often create dedicated BookTok display sections to capitalize on the trends. Quantifiable data, though sometimes proprietary and hard to consolidate across all retailers, consistently shows sharp sales spikes for titles once they achieve viral status on BookTok. For example, NPD BookScan data has frequently highlighted the correlation between BookTok trends and surges in print book sales in the US.

Beyond direct book sales, the rise of special editions, as mentioned, has become a lucrative market. These often premium-priced editions appeal to dedicated fans and collectors, demonstrating a willingness among BookTok readers to invest significantly in authors and series they love. Merchandise related to popular BookTok books—from art prints and clothing to themed candles and jewelry—also represents a growing ancillary market, often driven by indie creators on platforms like Etsy, further underscoring the deep engagement and consumer culture surrounding these literary worlds. This economic vitality is a clear indicator of BookTok's power to not only drive discovery but also to foster a highly motivated consumer base. However, the reliance on viral trends also introduces a degree of volatility into the market, with the potential for boom-and-bust cycles for specific subgenres or authors.

Navigating The New Landscape: Pressures, Pitfalls, And Sustainability For Authors And Publishers

While BookTok has opened exciting new doors, it also presents a complex array of pressures and potential pitfalls for both authors and publishers. For authors, the pressure to go viral, to conform to popular tropes, or to maintain a constant online presence can be immense. There's the risk of burnout, the challenge of managing sudden fame (and its attendant scrutiny), and the potential for creative vision to be compromised by the pursuit of trends. Concerns about the quality of rapidly produced books aiming to capitalize on fleeting trends are also valid, as editorial timelines might be compressed.

For publishers, the challenge lies in distinguishing genuine, sustainable trends from ephemeral hype. Investing heavily in a book based on BookTok buzz only to see interest wane quickly can be a costly mistake. There's also the ethical consideration of how to engage with BookTok creators, ensuring fair compensation for their promotional labor if formal partnerships are established. The rapid pace can also lead to a focus on frontlist titles that are currently trending, potentially at the expense of nurturing authors with slower-building careers or books that don't fit neatly into viral categories. The question of long-term sustainability is crucial: can a literary marketplace so heavily influenced by the rapid-fire, algorithmically driven trends of a single social media platform maintain its vibrancy and diversity in the long run? Or will it lead to a greater homogenization of content as everyone chases the same viral formula?

BookTok's remaking of authorship and publishing is a dynamic and ongoing process. It has undeniably democratized access to readership for some, breathed new life into backlist titles, and forced a traditional industry to innovate at an accelerated pace. The platform has proven that a passionate community, amplified by sophisticated algorithms, can exert an influence on par with, or even exceeding, that of established literary institutions. Yet, this new landscape is not without its shadows—the pressures on creators, the risks of market volatility, and the ongoing debate about the balance between commercial success and artistic integrity. As the industry and authors continue to navigate this terrain, the focus will increasingly be on how to harness BookTok's incredible power in a way that is sustainable, equitable, and ultimately enriches the literary ecosystem. Having explored the industry's transformation, the next chapter will turn to the heart of BookTok itself: the communities it fosters and the vibrant participatory culture that defines it.

CHAPTER 4: #BOOKTOKMADEMER EADIT

Community, Fandom, and
Participatory Culture

T he hashtag #BookTokMadeMeReadIt, emblazoned across countless videos and echoed in comment sections worldwide, is more than just a catchy phrase; it's a testament to the profound communal influence BookTok wields. Previous chapters have dissected the algorithmic mechanics that drive discovery (Chapter 1), the narrative elements that captivate readers (Chapter 2), and the seismic shifts this phenomenon has triggered within the publishing industry (Chapter 3). Now, we turn our gaze inward, to the very heart of BookTok: its people. This chapter explores how BookTok transcends its function as a mere recommendation engine to cultivate active, participatory fan communities. It argues that BookTok has become a vital cultural space where readers engage in collective meaning-making, express their passion through creative endeavors, and forge powerful emotional connections around shared literary experiences, thereby deepening their investment in the promoted genres and transforming solitary reading into a vibrant, social act.

More Than Readers: The Booktoker As Curator And Community Builder

At the forefront of BookTok communities are the creators themselves, often referred to as "BookTokers." These individuals are far more than passive readers; they are active curators, tastemakers, and community builders. While some boast follower counts in the millions, many influential voices operate on a smaller, more intimate scale, cultivating dedicated micro-communities around specific niches, genres, or authors. Their role extends beyond simply recommending books. They initiate discussions, pose thought-provoking questions, host live readalongs, and create challenges that encourage active participation. For instance, a BookToker might launch a "read a book from a debut author month" challenge, complete with suggested titles and a dedicated hashtag for participants to share their progress and thoughts.

These creators often develop a distinct voice and aesthetic, building a brand of trust and relatability with their audience. Their bookshelves become familiar backdrops, their reading habits a source of inspiration, and their emotional reactions a shared experience. By consistently engaging with their followers —replying to comments, acknowledging video responses (duets or stitches), and participating in broader community trends— BookTokers foster a sense of belonging and mutual respect. They are not distant celebrities but approachable peers, whose passion for literature is infectious. This accessibility is key to their influence. When a trusted BookToker raves about a new Romantasy novel, their endorsement carries the weight of a personal recommendation from a friend, making it far more compelling than a generic advertisement. They are, in essence, the modern-day equivalents of the enthusiastic bookseller who knows your taste or the friend whose literary judgment you implicitly trust, but operating on a global, algorithmically amplified scale.

Shared Language, Shared Experience: Tropes As Social Glue

As highlighted in Chapter 2, literary tropes play a crucial role in the appeal of BookTok-favored genres. Beyond their narrative function, these tropes also serve as a vital form of social glue within the community. Terms like "enemies-to-lovers," "found family," "morally grey anti-hero," "one bed," or "slow burn" are not just descriptive labels; they constitute a shared vernacular, a specialized language that signals common interests and facilitates immediate connection among users. When a BookToker posts a video captioned, "Looking for your best 'he falls first and harder' recs," they are tapping into a collective understanding and a pre-existing desire within the community.

This shared language allows for rapid and efficient communication of complex narrative expectations and emotional payoffs. It enables readers to quickly identify books that align with their preferences and to find other readers who share their specific tastes. Discussions often revolve around comparing how different authors execute a particular trope, debating the merits of various trope pairings, or celebrating iconic moments that exemplify a beloved trope. This collective engagement transforms individual reading preferences into a shared cultural experience. The joy is not just in reading a book with a favorite trope, but in discussing it, deconstructing it, and celebrating it with a like-minded community. This focus on tropes also lowers the barrier to entry for new community members; even if unfamiliar with specific titles, an understanding of popular tropes allows them to participate in conversations and discover new books.

From Consumption To Creation: Fan Art, Fan

Fiction, And Beyond

BookTok's participatory culture extends far beyond discussions and recommendations; it actively inspires a wide array of creative fan works. The platform is teeming with user-generated content that reinterprets, celebrates, and expands upon the literary worlds readers have come to love. This ranges from visually stunning "aesthetic edits" or "mood boards" that capture the essence of a book or character using curated images and music, to elaborate fan castings where users suggest actors to play their favorite characters in hypothetical adaptations.

Fan art is particularly prevalent, with artists sharing digital paintings, sketches, and animations inspired by scenes and characters from popular BookTok titles. Platforms like Instagram and Pinterest often serve as secondary hubs for this visual fandom, frequently linked back to BookTok discussions. While full-length fan fiction might be more commonly hosted on dedicated sites like Archive of Our Own (AO3) or Wattpad, BookTok often serves as a springboard, with users sharing plot bunnies, character analyses, or short written scenes that inspire longer works elsewhere. The comment sections of BookTok videos frequently become spaces for collaborative storytelling, with users riffing on "what if" scenarios or imagining future plot developments. This creative output signifies a deep level of engagement, where readers are not content to passively consume stories but are driven to actively participate in their cultural life, adding their own interpretations and expanding the narrative universes in meaningful ways. This co-creative energy is a hallmark of vibrant fandom, and BookTok has become a powerful catalyst for it.

The Global Bookshelf: Connecting Readers Across Borders

One of the most remarkable aspects of BookTok is its global

reach. While literary tastes can be culturally specific, BookTok has demonstrated a remarkable ability to connect readers across geographical and linguistic borders, creating a truly international "bookshelf." A Romantasy novel that goes viral in the United States can quickly find an eager audience in the United Kingdom, Australia, Canada, Germany, Brazil, the Philippines, and beyond, often leading to accelerated translation deals and international publishing successes.

Hashtags and trending sounds transcend language barriers to some extent, and the visual and emotional nature of BookTok content often communicates effectively even when creators and viewers don't share a common spoken language. English-language books frequently dominate global BookTok trends, but the platform also provides visibility for books from other linguistic traditions, particularly if they tap into universally appealing tropes and themes. This global connectivity fosters a sense of a worldwide reading community, where readers can share their passion for the same stories regardless of their location. It allows for the discovery of diverse perspectives and introduces readers to authors and narratives they might never have encountered through traditional, more regionally focused channels. This cross-cultural exchange, while still navigating the complexities of global media flows and linguistic dominance, enriches the reading experience and broadens the horizons of the BookTok community.

Challenges And Dynamics Within Booktok Communities

Like any large and dynamic online community, BookTok is not without its internal challenges and complexities. The very mechanisms that make it so effective at generating hype can also lead to issues. The pressure to keep up with rapidly changing trends can be exhausting for both creators and consumers. "Hype culture" can sometimes lead to unrealistic expectations for books, resulting in disappointment if a viral title doesn't live up to its massive online reputation. Differing opinions and critical discussions, while healthy, can sometimes devolve into negativity or "discourse" that becomes more about online conflict than literary engagement.

There can also be concerns about inclusivity and representation within the community. While BookTok has provided a platform for diverse voices, questions sometimes arise about which books and creators are amplified most effectively by the algorithm and whether certain perspectives remain marginalized. Issues of spoiler culture (the inadvertent or deliberate revealing of key plot points) are also a frequent point of contention, as are debates around the ethics of sponsored content and the perceived authenticity of recommendations. Managing these internal dynamics—fostering respectful debate, encouraging critical engagement alongside enthusiastic celebration, and ensuring a welcoming space for all readers—is an ongoing process for the BookTok community. These challenges, however, also underscore its vibrancy and its importance as a space where these crucial conversations about books and reading culture are actively taking place.

In essence, #BookTokMadeMeReadIt is a declaration of belonging, a marker of participation in a vast, interconnected web of readers who are collectively shaping literary tastes and experiences. BookTok has transformed reading from a predominantly solitary act into a deeply social and participatory one. It has built a global infrastructure for shared literary enthusiasm, complete with its own language, its own stars, and its own creative outputs. This vibrant community, with all its passion and its complexities, is not just reacting to trends but actively forging them, breathing life into stories and connecting readers in ways previously unimaginable. Having explored the powerful social dynamics that define this literary subculture, the final chapter will contemplate the broader cultural significance of this phenomenon, asking what the BookTok-driven Romantasy craze truly tells us about modern readership, our collective desires, and the evolving nature of culture in an algorithmically mediated world.

CHAPTER 5: BEYOND THE HYPE

*What the Romantasy Craze
Tells Us About Modern
Readership and Culture*

Having journeyed through the mechanics of BookTok's rise (Chapter 1), the narrative allure of its favored genres (Chapter 2), its revolutionary impact on publishing and authorship (Chapter 3), and the vibrant communities it fosters (Chapter 4), we arrive at a crucial juncture: to look beyond the immediate statistics and viral trends. What does the explosive popularity of Romantasy and related Speculative Fiction, as amplified and curated by BookTok, truly reveal about contemporary society, our collective psyche, and the evolving landscape of cultural consumption? This chapter argues that the BookTok-driven Romantasy surge is a significant cultural indicator, reflecting a profound contemporary yearning for immersive narratives that offer potent escapism from real-world complexities, a palpable sense of agency and empowerment (particularly resonating with female readers), intense emotional connection, and the solace of community in an increasingly fragmented digital world. Furthermore, the very platform of

TikTok, with its powerful algorithm, plays a complex and crucial role in this dynamic, acting as both a mirror reflecting pre-existing desires and a lens that actively shapes and magnifies them. Ultimately, this phenomenon is not just changing what people read, but is also forcing a necessary and ongoing re-evaluation of how literary value and success are defined and recognized in the 21st century.

Escapism In An Anxious Age: Finding Refuge In Fictional Worlds

One of the most evident drivers behind the Romantasy boom is a deep-seated desire for escapism. The early 2020s, the period marking BookTok's significant ascent, were characterized by unprecedented global anxieties: a pandemic, political polarization, economic uncertainties, and the looming specter of climate change. In such a context, the appeal of fictional worlds offering a complete departure from reality becomes immensely powerful. Romantasy, with its intricate magic systems, epic quests, and often clearly demarcated lines between good and evil (even when featuring morally grey characters), provides a rich tapestry into which readers can immerse themselves. These are not just stories; they are portals. The detailed world-building, from the dragon-filled skies of Navarre in *Fourth Wing* to the fae courts of Prythian in *A Court of Thorns and Roses*, offers a temporary reprieve from the often overwhelming and ambiguous challenges of modern life. This is not a new phenomenon—genre fiction has always offered escapist pleasures—but the intensity of this need and the scale at which BookTok has been able to satisfy it are noteworthy. The platform's visual nature, allowing creators to build "aesthetic" video collages that evoke the atmosphere of these worlds, further enhances this immersive quality, making the invitation to escape almost irresistible.

Empowerment Narratives And The Female Gaze In

Romantasy

A significant dimension of Romantasy's appeal, particularly for its predominantly female readership and creator base on BookTok, lies in its potent empowerment narratives. These stories frequently feature female protagonists who discover their strength, seize agency, and navigate treacherous circumstances, often in male-dominated fantastical societies. Characters like Aelin Galathynius (*Throne of Glass*) or Violet Sorrengail (*Fourth Wing*) undergo transformative journeys, evolving from positions of vulnerability or underestimation to become powerful figures who shape their own destinies and often the fate of their worlds. This resonates deeply with readers who may be navigating their own struggles for agency and recognition in various aspects of their lives.

Furthermore, many popular Romantasy narratives are arguably framed through a "female gaze," prioritizing female perspectives, desires, and emotional experiences, particularly in the development of romantic relationships. The focus is often on emotional intimacy, mutual respect (even amidst conflict), and the complex interiority of female characters, rather than solely on external action or a traditionally male-oriented perspective on conquest or heroism. The "morally grey" but fiercely devoted love interest, a staple of the genre, often represents a fantasy of being seen, understood, and cherished for one's strengths and flaws by a powerful partner who is, crucially, often willing to cede a degree of control or offer unwavering support. This focus on female empowerment and the validation of female desire contributes significantly to the genre's profound connection with its audience, offering narratives that not only entertain but also affirm and inspire.

The Search For Connection: Emotional Intensity And Community

In an era often characterized by digital detachment and social fragmentation, Romantasy and the BookTok community surrounding it offer powerful avenues for connection—both emotional and social. As discussed in Chapter 2, these narratives are engineered for high emotional intensity. They explore themes of profound love, devastating loss, unwavering loyalty, and epic sacrifice, allowing readers to experience a rich spectrum of feelings in a contained and cathartic way. The sharing of these intense emotional reactions on BookTok—the tears, the gasps, the outrage, the swooning—creates powerful bonds among users. It validates their feelings and transforms reading, often a solitary pursuit, into a shared emotional journey.

This shared emotional landscape is the bedrock of the BookTok community. As explored in Chapter 4, readers connect over shared favorite tropes, characters, and plot twists, forming global friendships and finding a sense of belonging. In a world where genuine connection can sometimes feel elusive, the BookTok community provides a space where individuals can bond deeply over a shared passion. This communal aspect is not merely a byproduct of the trend; it is integral to its power and persistence. The desire for stories that make one *feel* intensely is matched by the desire to share those feelings with others who understand, creating a powerful feedback loop of engagement and community reinforcement.

Nostalgia, Comfort Reads, And The "Binge" Culture

There's also an element of nostalgia and comfort in the appeal of Romantasy and certain speculative fiction tropes. For many readers, these genres evoke the immersive, plot-driven stories they may have loved in their youth, particularly within the Young Adult (YA) fantasy boom of the 2000s and 2010s. The clear narrative structures, the satisfying resolutions (even if hard-won), and the familiar beats of beloved tropes can provide a sense of comfort and predictability in an unpredictable world. These books often become "comfort reads," titles that readers return to repeatedly for the emotional solace they offer.

This ties into the prevalent "binge" culture that characterizes much of modern media consumption. Many popular Romantasy series are extensive, with multiple interconnected books, allowing readers to immerse themselves in a single world for extended periods. BookTok facilitates this binge-reading by making it easy to discover all the books in a series, find readalongs, and see others sharing their journey through multi-volume epics. The satisfaction of completing a long series, of living within a richly developed world for weeks or months, caters to a desire for sustained engagement and deep immersion, akin to binge-watching a popular television series. The often-cliffhanger endings and rapid plot pacing encourage this continuous consumption, making it hard to put a series down once started.

The Algorithm's Mirror: A Deep Dive Into Whether Booktok Reflects Or Shapes Our Desires

One of the most complex and critical questions arising from the BookTok phenomenon concerns the role of TikTok's algorithm: is it merely a passive mirror reflecting pre-existing reader desires, or is it an active agent that shapes and even creates those desires? The reality, as suggested by platform studies and reception theory, is likely a nuanced interplay of both. Drawing on Henry Jenkins' concept of "Convergence Culture," where media flows across platforms and audiences play a participatory role, BookTok exemplifies how user preferences and algorithmic promotion exist in a dynamic feedback loop.

Initially, the algorithm likely identified and amplified organic interest in Romantasy and specific tropes that were already resonating with a segment of readers. Users create content based on their genuine preferences; the algorithm observes engagement with this content (likes, shares, comments, watch time) and promotes similar content to users with comparable interaction histories. In this sense, it *reflects* existing tastes. However, once the algorithm identifies a trending topic, its powerful amplification capabilities can transform a niche interest into a mainstream phenomenon. By repeatedly exposing users to certain types of books, tropes, and aesthetic styles, it can normalize these preferences and create a sense of widespread appeal, thereby *shaping* desire. If a user's "For You Page" is consistently populated with emotional reviews of dragon-filled Romantasy, they are more likely to become curious and eventually seek out such books, even if it wasn't an initial strong preference. Publishers and authors, observing these algorithmically amplified trends, may then produce more content catering to these now highly visible desires, further solidifying the trend. This creates a cyclical relationship where user engagement, algorithmic promotion, and content creation continually influence each other. It's not a simple case of reflection or creation, but a complex, ongoing negotiation between user agency and algorithmic influence, where the platform both responds to and actively constructs popular taste.

Redefining Literary Value: How Booktok Challenges Traditional Metrics Of Success And Merit

Perhaps one of the most lasting impacts of the BookTok-Romantasy craze will be its challenge to traditional definitions of literary value and success. For centuries, literary merit has often been determined by a relatively small group of critics, academics, and award committees, frequently prioritizing qualities like stylistic innovation, thematic complexity, and "seriousness" of purpose. Commercial success, particularly in genre fiction, has sometimes been viewed with suspicion, as if popularity inherently precludes literary worth.

BookTok disrupts this hierarchy by championing books based on entirely different criteria: emotional impact, readability, trope satisfaction, and the ability to foster community and passionate discussion. Success on BookTok is measured in likes, shares, viral trends, and ultimately, sales figures driven by genuine reader enthusiasm rather than critical accolades. This is forcing a broader conversation about what constitutes "good" literature and who gets to decide. Is a book that brings immense joy, comfort, and a sense of community to millions of readers less valuable than a critically acclaimed novel that is read by a much smaller audience? BookTok implicitly argues no. It champions the reader's experience as the ultimate arbiter of value, suggesting that the power of a story to connect, to move, and to create shared meaning is a legitimate, and perhaps paramount, form of literary merit. This doesn't mean that traditional literary criticism becomes irrelevant, but it does mean that its monopoly on defining value is being seriously contested. The BookTok phenomenon suggests a more democratized, reader-centric model of literary valuation, where emotional resonance and communal engagement are powerful currencies.

The Romantasy craze, amplified and curated by BookTok, is far more than a fleeting literary fad. It is a cultural barometer, reflecting deep-seated contemporary desires for escapism from an anxious world, for narratives of empowerment that validate and inspire, and for the profound emotional and social connections that stories can forge. It highlights the intricate dance between human desire and algorithmic influence, demonstrating how technology can both mirror and mold our cultural appetites. Most significantly, it throws down a gauntlet to traditional notions of literary worth, championing a vision of literature where the reader's emotional journey and the power of shared experience are paramount. As we move towards the conclusion of this exploration, it is clear that the echoes of the algorithm's muse will resonate through the halls of publishing, and in the hearts of readers, for a long time to come, prompting an ongoing re-evaluation of how stories are created, discovered, and cherished in our modern world.

CONCLUSION

The Enduring Echo of the Algorithm's Muse

O ur journey through the vibrant, tumultuous, and undeniably influential world of BookTok and its reigning genres, particularly Romantasy, has traversed a landscape reshaped by algorithms, fueled by passionate communities, and reflective of profound contemporary desires. We have witnessed how a social media platform, initially an unlikely contender in the literary sphere, has risen to become a formidable force, its "For You Page" acting as a digital kingmaker, its users the enthusiastic arbiters of new literary canons. This book has argued that TikTok's BookTok community has not merely influenced the contemporary fiction landscape but has fundamentally reshaped it. By masterfully leveraging emotionally resonant, visually driven user-generated content and the unparalleled reach of algorithmic amplification, BookTok has become an unprecedented catalyst for the surge in Romantasy and related Speculative Fiction. In doing so, it has not only created viral bestsellers and cultivated fervent global fanbases but has also elevated new and diverse authorial voices, all while mirroring and responding to a deep-seated cultural yearning for immersive escapism, intense emotional connection, and a powerful sense of shared experience. Crucially, this phenomenon has ignited a necessary and ongoing re-evaluation of how we define literary success and artistic merit in the 21st century.

Throughout these chapters, we have pieced together the mosaic of BookTok's impact. We began in Chapter 1, "The Rise of the Algorithm's Muse," by dissecting the unique ecosystem of TikTok itself—its potent algorithm, the compelling anatomy of its short-form video content, and the organic emergence of a community that transformed personal reading experiences into public declarations. We saw how authenticity, or at least its potent perception, became the currency of trust, allowing BookTok to bypass traditional gatekeepers. Chapter 2, "Dragons, Desire, and Dark Academia," then plunged into the heart of the narratives themselves, deconstructing the irresistible appeal of Romantasy and its speculative cousins. We explored how specific tropes, compelling character archetypes, rich world-building, and the promise of profound emotional intensity resonated so deeply, fulfilling reader desires for escapism, empowerment, and connection, while also acknowledging the critical conversations these trends inspire regarding originality and depth.

The shockwaves of this appeal were examined in Chapter 3, "From Viral Videos to Bestseller Lists," which charted BookTok's revolutionary impact on the staid structures of authorship and publishing. We witnessed the rise of indie sensations, the revival of backlist Cinderellas, and the scramble of an entire industry to adapt to new marketing paradigms, acquisition strategies, and the accelerated pace of digitally-native trends. This chapter highlighted both the democratization of opportunity and the new pressures faced by authors and publishers alike. Chapter 4, "#BookTokMadeMeReadIt," shifted focus to the vibrant soul of the movement: its community. We explored how BookTok fosters a dynamic participatory culture, transforming readers into curators, critics, and creators in their own right, united by a shared language of tropes and a collective passion that turns solitary reading into a global, social event. Finally, Chapter 5, "Beyond the Hype," stepped back to interpret the broader cultural significance of the Romantasy craze, viewing it as a mirror reflecting contemporary anxieties and aspirations—our yearning for refuge, our search for agency, our hunger for connection—and considered the complex interplay of the "algorithm's mirror," questioning how much it reflects versus how much it shapes our literary desires, ultimately challenging entrenched notions of literary value.

The legacy of the BookTok phenomenon, particularly during its formative surge from early 2022 to early 2025, is multifaceted and will undoubtedly continue to evolve. For the future of literature, it signals a lasting shift in discovery. While traditional review outlets and awards will retain their place, the power of peer-to-peer recommendation, amplified by social algorithms, is now an undeniable and likely permanent fixture in how readers find books. This may lead to a more diverse array of voices reaching mainstream audiences, particularly those adept at leveraging these new platforms, but it also raises questions about the long-term visibility of works that don't easily lend themselves to viral video formats. For the publishing industry, the adaptation will continue. Agility, a deeper understanding of digital communities, and a willingness to embrace non-traditional pathways to success will be paramount. The relationship between authors, publishers, and readers has become more direct, more interactive, and in many ways, more transparent, though also laden with new expectations for constant engagement.

The online communities forged on BookTok, and similar platforms that may arise, demonstrate the enduring human need for shared stories and collective meaning-making. These digital campfires offer connection and validation, but also highlight the complexities of online discourse, including the management of hype, the potential for echo chambers, and the challenges of fostering inclusive and respectful dialogue. The redefinition of literary value is perhaps BookTok's most profound, and potentially contentious, legacy. The platform has unequivocally shown that commercial success driven by genuine reader passion can exist independently of, and sometimes in defiance of, traditional critical acclaim. It champions emotional impact, immersive pleasure, and communal resonance as legitimate, powerful metrics of a book's worth. This doesn't negate the importance of literary craft or thematic depth, but it broadens the conversation, forcing us to consider a more inclusive and reader-centric understanding of what makes a book "good" or "important."

It is crucial to acknowledge the dynamic nature of TikTok and the digital landscape. Trends will shift, new platforms may emerge, and the specific genres dominating BookTok today might evolve or be supplanted tomorrow. The very algorithm that propelled Romantasy to its zenith is a constantly learning, ever-changing entity. However, the fundamental principles uncovered during BookTok's rise—the power of authentic emotional connection, the appeal of immersive narrative, the drive for community, and the democratizing potential of user-driven content amplified by technology—will likely endure. The "Algorithm's Muse," in whatever form it takes next, will continue to sing, and the literary world will need to keep listening.

Embarking on this analysis has been a journey into the heart of contemporary reading culture, a fascinating intersection of age-old storytelling traditions and cutting-edge digital technology. It has been a study of how quickly and profoundly our methods of sharing and celebrating literature can change, yet how constant our fundamental human need for stories remains. The passion, creativity, and sheer joy exuded by the BookTok community are infectious, and their collective ability to reshape an industry is nothing short of remarkable. While critical questions about quality, sustainability, and the pressures of viral culture are vital and ongoing, one cannot deny the energy and enthusiasm BookTok has injected into the world of books. It has made reading visibly cool, intensely social, and undeniably exciting for a new generation, and for that alone, its echo will be long-lasting. The algorithm may provide the stage, but it is the human heart, in its eternal quest for connection and meaning through stories, that truly directs the show.

GLOSSARY

This glossary provides definitions for key terms used throughout *The Algorithm's Muse: How TikTok's BookTok Community Redefined Literary Success and Made Romantasy Rule*. These terms relate to the BookTok community, the TikTok platform, publishing, literary genres, and broader cultural concepts discussed in the book.

Aesthetic Edit (or Mood Board)
A type of video or visual collage, popular on BookTok, that uses curated images, video clips, and music to evoke the specific mood, atmosphere, or visual style of a book, character, or setting.

Algorithm (TikTok)
The complex computational system used by TikTok to curate and recommend content to users on their "For You Page." It analyzes user interactions (likes, shares, comments, watch time) to personalize the content feed.

Algorithm's Muse
A term coined in this book to describe the powerful, often unseen influence of social media algorithms (specifically TikTok's) in shaping literary trends, popularizing authors, and anointing certain genres or books as cultural phenomena. It refers to the way the algorithm seems to "inspire" or dictate success.

ARC (Advance Reader Copy)
A pre-publication version of a book sent to reviewers, influencers (including BookTokers), and booksellers for review and promotional purposes before its official release date.

Authenticity (on BookTok)

A perceived quality of genuineness and sincerity in BookTok content, where creators share honest, often unfiltered emotional reactions and personal opinions about books. This is a key factor in the trustworthiness and persuasive power of BookTok recommendations.

Backlist (Titles)

Books that are not newly published but are still in print and available for sale. BookTok has shown a significant ability to revive interest in and drive sales for backlist titles.

Bestseller List

A list of books that have sold the most copies in a given period, such as those compiled by The New York Times or USA Today. BookTok has become a major driver for books appearing on these lists.

Binge Culture / Binge-Reading

A pattern of consumption characterized by reading multiple books in a series or by a particular author in rapid succession, often driven by immersive worlds and compelling narratives.

BookTok

A subcommunity on the social media platform TikTok dedicated to books and reading. Users share reviews, recommendations, reactions, and other creative content related to literature.

BookToker

A TikTok user who creates and shares content within the BookTok community.

Comfort Read

A book or series that a reader returns to for feelings of familiarity, solace, and emotional comfort, often due to beloved characters, predictable plot structures, or positive emotional payoffs.

Content Creator

An individual who produces and shares digital content (videos, posts, etc.) on social media platforms like TikTok.

Convergence Culture
A term coined by Henry Jenkins describing the flow of content across multiple media platforms, the cooperation between multiple media industries, and the migratory behavior of media audiences who will go almost anywhere in search of the kinds of entertainment experiences they want.

Dark Academia
A subgenre of fiction and an aesthetic characterized by themes of elite education, classic literature, the pursuit of knowledge (often forbidden or dangerous), and settings like old universities, libraries, and boarding schools. It often incorporates elements of mystery, tragedy, and sometimes the supernatural or fantastical.

Duet (TikTok Feature)
A TikTok feature that allows a user to create a video that appears side-by-side with another user's video, often used for reactions, collaborations, or responses.

Dystopian Romance
A subgenre of speculative fiction that blends dystopian themes (societies characterized by oppression, control, and often environmental ruin) with a central romantic plotline where characters find love while struggling against the oppressive system.

Emotional Intensity / Emotional Resonance
The quality of a narrative that evokes strong feelings in the reader, such as joy, sorrow, anger, or excitement. This is a highly valued characteristic in books popular on BookTok.

Empowerment Narratives
Stories that focus on characters, often female, who gain agency, overcome adversity, and discover their personal strength and power.

Enemies-to-Lovers (Trope)
A popular romantic trope where two characters who initially dislike or are openly hostile towards each other gradually develop romantic feelings.

Escapism
The tendency to seek distraction and relief from unpleasant realities, especially by seeking entertainment or engaging in fantasy. Immersive fictional worlds are a key form of escapism for many readers.

Fan Art
Artwork created by fans of a particular work of fiction (such as a book or series), depicting characters, scenes, or concepts from that work.

Fan Fiction
Fictional stories written by fans, featuring characters and settings from an original work of fiction.

Fandom
A community of fans of a particular person, team, fictional series, etc., often engaging in collective activities, discussions, and creative expressions related to their shared interest.

Female Gaze
A perspective in art and literature that prioritizes female viewpoints, experiences, and desires, often as a counterpoint to the traditionally dominant male gaze. In Romantasy, this can manifest in the focus on female protagonists' emotional journeys and agency in romantic relationships.

For You Page (FYP)
The main content feed on TikTok, algorithmically curated and personalized for each user, showcasing videos from creators they may or may not follow. It is a primary driver of content discovery on the platform.

Found Family (Trope)
A narrative trope where a group of unrelated characters form deep, supportive, family-like bonds, often due to shared experiences, mutual support, or common goals.

Forced Proximity (Trope)
A romantic trope where characters are forced into close physical contact or a shared space, leading to increased tension, vulnerability, and often the development of romantic feelings.

Frontlist (Titles)
Newly published books.

Gatekeepers (Literary)
Individuals or institutions (such as critics, publishers, agents, award committees) that traditionally controlled access to publication and influenced which books achieved recognition and success.

Genre Homogenization
The potential tendency for books within a popular genre to become increasingly similar in terms of plot, tropes, and character archetypes, often due to market pressures to replicate successful formulas.

Hashtag (#)
A word or phrase preceded by a hash sign (#), used on social media platforms to identify messages on a specific topic and allow users to easily find content related to that topic.

Hype / Hype Culture
Intense excitement, promotion, and widespread discussion surrounding a particular product, event, or trend, often generated and amplified by social media.

Indie Author / Independent Author
An author who publishes their work without a traditional publishing house, often managing the editing, design,

distribution, and marketing themselves (self-publishing) or through small, independent presses.

Literary Value / Literary Merit
The perceived quality, importance, or artistic worth of a literary work. Traditional definitions often emphasize stylistic innovation, thematic depth, and critical acclaim, while BookTok often prioritizes emotional impact and reader enjoyment.

Morally Grey Character / Anti-Hero (Archetype)
A protagonist or prominent character who has ambiguous moral qualities, operates outside conventional ethical codes, or performs questionable actions, yet may still evoke sympathy or admiration from the reader.

Mythological Retelling
A literary work that reinterprets or reimagines existing myths, legends, or folklore, often from a new perspective or with a contemporary sensibility.

One Bed Trope
A specific instance of forced proximity where characters are compelled to share a single bed, typically leading to romantic or comedic tension.

Participatory Culture
A culture in which private individuals (the public) do not act as consumers only, but also as contributors or producers (prosumers). BookTok is a prime example, with users actively creating content, shaping discussions, and influencing trends.

Platform Studies
An academic field that investigates the cultural, social, political, and economic impact of digital platforms (like social media sites, search engines, etc.) and their underlying infrastructures and algorithms.

Portmanteau
A word blending the sounds and combining the meanings of two

others (e.g., "Romantasy" from "Romance" and "Fantasy").

Reader-Centric
An approach to literature or literary analysis that prioritizes the reader's experience, interpretation, and emotional response to a text.

Reception Theory
A version of reader-response literary theory that emphasizes the reader's active role in creating meaning from a literary text. It considers how texts are received and interpreted by different audiences at different times.

Romantasy
A subgenre of fiction that blends elements of romance and fantasy, where the romantic plot and the fantastical plot are typically deeply intertwined and integral to the overall narrative.

Shelfie
A photograph of a bookshelf or collection of books, often shared on social media to showcase one's reading tastes or library.

Slow Burn (Trope)
A romantic trope where the development of romantic feelings between characters is gradual and drawn out over a significant portion of the narrative, building anticipation and tension.

Social Algorithm
See Algorithm (TikTok). Refers to the algorithms used by social media platforms to filter, rank, and recommend content.

Special Edition (Books)
Versions of books produced with unique features not found in standard editions, such as sprayed edges, custom cover art, foiled details, author signatures, or bonus content, often targeted at collectors and dedicated fans.

Speculative Fiction
A broad literary genre encompassing fiction with supernatural,

fantastical, futuristic, or other imaginative elements that depart from reality. Subgenres include fantasy, science fiction, horror, dystopian fiction, and more.

Stitch (TikTok Feature)
A TikTok feature that allows users to clip and integrate moments from another user's video into their own, often used for commentary, responses, or building upon existing content.

Strong Female Protagonist (Archetype)
A leading female character who demonstrates agency, resilience, capability, and often plays a pivotal role in driving the plot and overcoming challenges.

Taste-Makers
Individuals or groups whose opinions and preferences significantly influence what becomes popular or fashionable within a particular cultural domain, such as literature.

Trending Sound
An audio clip—music, dialogue snippet, or original sound—that becomes popular on TikTok and is widely used by creators in their videos.

Trope
A common or overused theme, character, plot device, or narrative convention in literature or storytelling. On BookTok, tropes are often celebrated and used as a way to categorize and recommend books based on reader preferences.

Trope Fatigue
A feeling of weariness or disinterest among readers resulting from the perceived overuse or repetitive implementation of popular literary tropes.

User-Generated Content (UGC)
Any form of content—such as videos, images, text, audio—that is created and shared by users of online platforms rather than by the platform owners or traditional media producers.

Viral / Virality

The tendency of an image, video, piece of information, or other content to be circulated rapidly and widely from one internet user to another.

World-Building

The process of constructing an imaginary world, often associated with speculative fiction, complete with its own history, geography, culture, rules, and inhabitants.

YA (Young Adult)

A category of fiction written for readers aged approximately 12 to 18, though often read by adults as well. It frequently explores themes of identity, coming-of-age, and navigating complex social worlds.

BIBLIOGRAPHY

This bibliography provides a representative list of primary literary texts, academic works, industry publications, media reports, and online resources that inform the analysis presented in *The Algorithm's Muse: How TikTok's BookTok Community Redefined Literary Success and Made Romantasy Rule*. Given the dynamic nature of online content and the broad scope of the phenomenon, this list is illustrative rather than exhaustive.

Key Literary Texts
Armentrout, Jennifer L. *From Blood and Ash*. Blue Box Press, 2020.
Bardugo, Leigh. *Six of Crows*. Henry Holt and Co., 2015.
Blake, Olivie. *The Atlas Six*. Self-published, 2020; Tor Books, 2022.
Hoover, Colleen. *It Ends With Us*. Atria Books, 2016.
Maas, Sarah J. *A Court of Thorns and Roses*. Bloomsbury, 2015.
Maas, Sarah J. *Throne of Glass*. Bloomsbury, 2012.
Mafi, Tahereh. *Shatter Me*. HarperCollins, 2011.
Miller, Madeline. *Circe*. Little, Brown and Company, 2018.
Roberts, Lauren. *Powerless*. Self-published, 2023; Simon & Schuster, 2023.
Saint, Jennifer. *Ariadne*. Flatiron Books, 2021.
St. Clair, Scarlett. *A Touch of Darkness*. Self-published, 2019.
Yarros, Rebecca. *Fourth Wing*. Red Tower Books (Entangled Publishing), 2023.
Yarros, Rebecca. *Iron Flame*. Red Tower Books (Entangled Publishing), 2023.

Academic Works & Theoretical Frameworks
Baym, Nancy K. *Personal Connections in the Digital Age*. Polity Press, 2010.

Bruns, Axel. *Blogs, Wikipedia, Second Life, and Beyond: From Production to Produsage*. Peter Lang, 2008.

Burgess, Jean, and Joshua Green. *YouTube: Online Video and Participatory Culture*. Polity Press, 2018.

Couldry, Nick, and Andreas Hepp. *The Mediated Construction of Reality*. Polity Press, 2017.

Fish, Stanley. *Is There a Text in This Class? The Authority of Interpretive Communities*. Harvard University Press, 1980.

Fiske, John. *Understanding Popular Culture*. Routledge, 1989.

Gillespie, Tarleton. *Custodians of the Internet: Platforms, Content Moderation, and the Hidden Decisions That Shape Social Media*. Yale University Press, 2018.

Hall, Stuart. *Representation: Cultural Representations and Signifying Practices*. Sage Publications, 1997.

Jauss, Hans Robert. *Toward an Aesthetic of Reception*. University of Minnesota Press, 1982.

Jenkins, Henry. *Convergence Culture: Where Old and New Media Collide*. New York University Press, 2006.

Jenkins, Henry. *Textual Poachers: Television Fans & Participatory Culture*. Routledge, 1992.

Pariser, Eli. *The Filter Bubble: What the Internet Is Hiding from You*. Penguin Press, 2011.

Radway, Janice A. *Reading the Romance: Women, Patriarchy, and Popular Literature*. University of North Carolina Press, 1984.

Squire, John. *The New Gatekeepers: Social Media, Algorithms, and the Future of Book Publishing*. (Placeholder for a hypothetical future academic work).

Thompson, John B. *Merchants of Culture: The Publishing Business in the Twenty-First Century*. Polity Press, 2010.

Turkle, Sherry. *Alone Together: Why We Expect More from Technology and Less from Each Other*. Basic Books, 2011.

Van Dijck, José. *The Culture of Connectivity: A Critical History of Social Media*. Oxford University Press, 2013.

Zuboff, Shoshana. *The Age of Surveillance Capitalism: The Fight for a Human Future at the New Frontier of Power*. PublicAffairs, 2019.

Industry Publications & Media Reports

The Bookseller. Various articles covering BookTok trends, sales impacts, and publisher strategies. (Specific articles would be cited with dates and titles in a full research project).

NPD BookScan (and its successor Circana BookScan). Industry sales data reports.

Publishers Weekly. Numerous articles, features, and news items on the impact of BookTok on publishing, author careers, and genre trends. (Specific articles would be cited).

Reports and articles from major news outlets such as *The New York Times, The Guardian, The Wall Street Journal, Vox, Wired,* etc., covering the BookTok phenomenon. (Specific articles, authors, and dates would be cited). For example:

Harris, Elizabeth A. "How TikTok Became a Best-Seller Machine." *The New York Times.* (Illustrative example of a likely article title and source).

Paul, Kari. "The Rise of #BookTok: How a TikTok Trend Is Driving Book Sales." *The Guardian.* (Illustrative example).

Online Sources & Key BookTok Accounts

TikTok Platform: Direct observation of trends, hashtags (e.g., #BookTok, #Romantasy, #FourthWing, #ACOTAR), and viral video content. (Specific URLs and access dates would be meticulously recorded in a research log).

Influential BookTok Creator Accounts: Analysis of content from established and emerging BookTok creators who have significantly shaped genre trends and discussions. Examples of early/foundational accounts often cited include (but are not limited to, and with the understanding that influence shifts):

@aymansbooks

@caitsbooks

@abbysbooks

(And numerous others relevant to specific trends and periods analyzed).

Author TikTok Accounts: Publicly available content from authors active on TikTok (e.g., Rebecca Yarros, Sarah J. Maas (fan-run or publisher-run accounts if applicable), Lauren Roberts, Olivie Blake).

Goodreads and StoryGraph: Reader reviews, community discussions, and book-specific forums related to titles popularized on BookTok.

Reddit: Subreddits such as r/RomanceBooks, r/Fantasy, r/BookTok, and specific author/series subreddits for community discussions and sentiment analysis.

ACKNOWLEDGEMENTS

The creation of a book, even one that explores the fast-paced digital world, is rarely a solitary endeavor. While the name on the cover is singular, the journey to completion is often supported by a multitude of individuals and communities, both seen and unseen. It is with deep gratitude that I acknowledge those who have contributed, in various ways, to the development and realization of *The Algorithm's Muse*.

First and foremost, I extend my sincere thanks to the vibrant and dynamic BookTok community. Your passion, creativity, and willingness to share your love for literature in such innovative ways were the primary inspiration for this work. To the countless creators who craft insightful, humorous, and emotionally resonant videos, and to the engaged readers who participate in discussions and build connections around shared stories: thank you for creating such a fascinating cultural phenomenon worthy of exploration. While individual names are too numerous to list, your collective voice is the heartbeat of this book.

I am indebted to the authors whose works are discussed within these pages. Your storytelling prowess and ability to craft worlds that captivate millions form the bedrock of the trends analyzed herein. Thank you for your contributions to literature and for engaging with your readers in such accessible ways.

To the publishing professionals—editors, agents, marketers, and publicists—who navigate the ever-evolving landscape of the book industry, your insights, whether shared directly or through industry publications, have been invaluable. Your efforts to bring stories to readers, and your adaptability in the face of new media trends, are crucial to the literary ecosystem.

My gratitude also extends to the scholars and researchers in media studies, cultural studies, literary studies, and platform studies. Your theoretical frameworks and analytical work provide essential tools for understanding the complex interplay between technology, culture, and society. The works cited in the bibliography represent just a fraction of the intellectual labor that has informed my thinking.

For their unwavering support and understanding during the writing process, I thank my friends and family. Your patience during periods of intense focus and your willingness to listen to endless musings on algorithms and Romantasy have meant more than words can say.

Finally, to the reader: thank you for embarking on this exploration. It is my hope that this book offers a useful lens through which to view the remarkable ways in which technology and community are reshaping our relationship with literature, and that it sparks further curiosity about the stories we share and the platforms that connect us.

Azirion Jase, May 2025.

ABOUT THE AUTHOR

Azirion Jase

Just an ordinary soul, cloaked in the quiet of everyday life, yet consumed by an unshakable obsession with the fantastical. My heart beats for the stories that dance in the shadows of my imagination—untamed, enigmatic, and yearning to be shared.

There is nothing remarkable about me, no grand achievements to boast of, only a strange and restless fire that compels me to weave worlds from whispers and dreams. I offer these creations with hope—that they might stir something within you, a spark of wonder, a touch of mystery, or a feeling that lingers long after the last word fades.

And when I give voice to reality, I pour forth all that I am and all that I've gathered from the scattered hours of my life, leaving no shadow unexplored, no truth unsought.